Flirtology

100 ways
to release your
inner flirt

© Text copyright 2004 Anita Naik

Published in Great Britain in 2004
by Hodder Children's Books

Editor: Katie Sergeant
Design by Fiona Webb
Cover design: Hodder Children's Books

The right of Anita Naik to be identified as the author of the
Work has been asserted by her in accordance with the
Copyright, Designs and Patents Act 1988.

10 9 8 7 6 5 4 3 2 1

A catalogue record for this book is available from the British
Library.

ISBN: 0340881445

Printed by Bookmarque Ltd, Croydon, Surrey

The paper and board used in this paperback by Hodder
Children's Books are natural recyclable products made from
wood grown in sustainable forests. The manufacturing
processes conform to the environmental regulations of the
country of origin.

Hodder Children's Books
a division of Hodder Headline Limited
338 Euston Road
London NW1 3BH

Flirtology

Anita Naik

*Hodder
Children's
Books*

a division of Hodder Headline Limited

For Cassie and Nell –
for when you're older and in need
of some boy advice

Wise up
to flirting

Contrary to popular opinion there's nothing sleazy about flirting. It's a basic human instinct designed to help us attract a partner. If you've ever made eyes across a room, smiled at a handsome stranger, or even teased a guy to make them laugh, you've flirted.

Use it
or
lose it

Not all of us are natural flirts
but the good news is everyone
has an inner flirt battling to
get out. However, it takes time
to build up your flirt muscles
so help yourself by exercising them
daily. Start right now by smiling at
the first fanciable man you spot.

Think about how you flirt

How guys receive your flirting signals:

- 55% comes from your body language
- 38% from the way your voice sounds
  – tone, voice, and attitude
- 7% from what you actually say.

The power of flirting lies not in how pretty or clever you are, but in the signals you send out. Your friends may all think you're the funniest and most gorgeous person on earth, but this means nothing if you go to pieces when a boy talks to you. Become aware of what you're doing when boys approach you (ask your best friend).

Be
Positive

If you're constantly whining
about not having a boyfriend,
you're squashing your inner flirt.
Our brain believes what we tell it.
Complain that all boys are rubbish
and you'll never notice the great
guys. Think positive and activate
your inner flirt.

Don't be
afraid to
take risks

Successful flirts take risks. Wait for someone else to make the first move, and you'll also be waiting to be asked out, kissed and called. Those who try, get results. If you spot someone you like, don't wait by the sidelines, jump in – what have you got to lose?

Good mood
good flirt

Good flirts are fun. This
doesn't mean you have to crack
a joke every five minutes, but it
means being in a good mood when
you flirt (or else it will backfire).
If you're about to go out, a good
trick is to put on your favourite
CD, turn it up and dance wildly
round your room for five minutes.
Then take a deep breath and
hit the road.

Take a
deep breath

To find your courage:

- just go for it
- don't try to predict the outcome
- if you get knocked back try again
  with someone else.

Despite what people tell you,
you don't need props to give
you courage. The best way to
feel brave is to simply take a
deep breath and give it a go.
Keep practising your technique
and you'll find the more you flirt,
the less afraid you'll feel about it
and the more courageous you'll be.

Pick the
right flirting
venue

Studies show that schools,
colleges, coffee shops and fast
food places are all excellent flirt
locations. This is because here
people are more open to meeting
others and willing to chat.
Bad locations are restaurants
and the cinema where people
prefer to be left alone.

Aim your
beam wide

Always start with your flirt
gaze on full beam and let it sweep
over every guy in the room before
you narrow it down to one person.
Sometimes you'll find Mr Right
in five seconds, but other times it
will take a few tries. Scan with
a smile on your face and you'll
find someone before long.

Smile on the lookout

How to smile the right way:

- imagine for a second the nicest compliment someone ever gave you and let it bring a grin to your face
- or imagine a smiley mouth working itself up from your stomach, up your body into your face and eyes.

Walk around staring at your feet and all you'll see are the cracks in the pavement. Look up and the dating possibilities become apparent. To boost your flirt power, make eye contact with boys you fancy as you walk down the street. Look them in the eye, smile, carry on walking and then look back to see if they've picked up your signals (9 times out of 10 they'll be looking back too).

Make up
your mind

All it takes is 90 seconds to
decide if you fancy someone or
not, so make those 90 seconds
count! Before you hotfoot it over,
check out his body language.
If he's smiling, standing with his
shoulders back and looking at you,
then he's ready to flirt.

The best
flirt tip in
the world

The perfect tip for letting
someone know you like them is
to look at someone until they look
at you, hold their gaze for under
a second and then look away.
Follow it up with a smile within
another second and you'll have
them hooked.

Don't
give up

Don't give up if you don't
get immediate results from
your flirting techniques.
While your aim is to attract
someone's attention, if they're
not interested or misread your
signals learn from your mistakes
and move on. Getting stuck on
rejection is boring for your friends,
dull for you and will kill your
flirting bug.

Learn from a master flirt

Flirt tips:

- don't copy other people's moves exactly – pick up some helpful hints that you can adapt
- watch how people keep the conversation going (verbal signs) and how they make it clear that they want more (tactile signals).

If you're hopeless at flirting,
it pays to spend some time
watching an expert at work.
Choose a friend whose flirt style
you admire, or go somewhere like
a coffee shop and people watch.
If that fails pick your favourite
chick-flick movie and note how
the main character flirts and
gets her guy.

Forget rejection

Remember:

- everyone has been rejected by someone in their lifetime
- rejection is rarely about you. It's often more about the other person.

Re-live your dating failures and all you'll do is put yourself through rejection over and over again. Instead of thinking about the past, move on. Remember you have to be in it to win it (i.e. if you don't try, you'll never date anyone).

Dress
to impress

Beauty is in the eye of the
beholder and yes, personality
should count, but you can't run
away from the fact that appearance
also counts. That doesn't mean
you have to look like a supermodel
to get a date but it does mean
making the most of yourself.
Make yourself look gorgeous
and you'll feel fantastic.

Make sure
your clothes
reflect who
you are

You think guys like girls who dress like sexy divas, but is a micro mini and wonderbra really YOU? Are these the signals you want to give someone? Dressing against your personality is a flirting no-no. Always wear what you feel gives out the right signals for your personality (though don't let shyness hide your light under a black baggy jumper).

Stand up straight

Improve your posture:

- pull in your stomach (imagine your bellybutton pulling back towards your spine)
- drop your shoulders (to get rid of that hunched look)
- imagine your chest bone pulling upwards (drop your ribs).

To literally stand out in a crowd
all it takes is good posture.
Studies show that before you've
even spoken a word, the way you
stand counts for over 80% of
someone's first impression of you.
So don't hunch your shoulders,
slouch at the table and/or let
everything hang out.

Hang around
with happy
people

A study from the US has
shown that happiness is infectious.
So to boost your inner flirt power,
always hang around with people
who look and act happy. Scientists
have also found that people find it
hard to ignore and walk away from
happy people, so grab his attention
by smiling and having some fun.

Be aware
when someone's
flirting with you

Don't get so wrapped up in
your own flirting techniques that
you don't notice when someone's
flirting with you. Hints that
someone likes you include:
suddenly always being around
your favourite haunts, trying
to make you laugh all the time,
or trying to get your attention
by being silly.

Give him an
opportunity

Screaming loudly with your
mates may make a guy look
your way, but it won't make him
come over and chat you up.
Studies show men are put off by
groups of loud women, so if your
aim is to get a date make sure that
you break away from your group
and give him a chance to approach
you on your own.

Watch your
flirtometer

Flirting is addictive and when you get good at it, it's tempting to turn it on with everyone. However, flirting with people like your best friend's dad, your teacher, your sister's boyfriend etc. is not only embarrassing but also inappropriate. Stick to single guys in your age range and it will stop you landing in hot water with someone.

Flirt for fun
not for frolics

Being overly suggestive is not
the same as flirting. While there
is a bit of a sexual undertone
to flirting, being OTT about
bodies, being smutty, or implying
you're wilder than you are,
suggests you want more from a
guy than a simple evening of
genuine fun flirting.

The
eyebrow flash

This is an effective flirting tool
in a crowded party. Basically
it involves raising your eyebrows
very briefly (for less than a
second) to make the person
who catches it think he
knows you. Add a smile
and he'll come over.

Make
your move

He smiles, you smile back.
You look, he looks back, you grin,
he grins... stop it now and get
over there! Guys are notoriously
thick-skinned about getting the
message, which means if he's
giving you signals but not moving
you have to go to him.

Notice his signals

He likes you when:

- he singles you out from a group
- he asks you questions about yourself
- he accidentally finds ways to brush against you.

You can have the best flirting
tools in the world but if you
don't know how to read his signals
you'll still be hopeless at flirting.
I-like-you signals are moving
closer to you, nodding, and
accidental-on-purpose touching.
Not-interested signals are looking
around while you are speaking,
keeping a distance from you and
calling you someone else's name!

Ask
intelligent
questions

Saying, "So do you like me?"
is a good flirting starter,
but follow it up with equally
me-me-me questions and you'll
scare him away. The key is to act
interested, and be interesting!
If you're stuck for what to say,
think of questions that you like
to be asked, and ask him those.

Be positive
about yourself

How to be positive:

- talk about your good traits – it's not boasting to say you're good at something
- emphasise your good points – if you have a nice smile, wear earrings to draw his attention to your face.

Don't fish for compliments
by putting yourself down.
Say you're fat and boring enough
times in one conversation and
the person you're talking to
will start to believe you.
Instead be positive to get a
positive response (notice how
boys never put themselves down).

Perfect
your pose

Watch your stance. Hovering
over a guy who is sitting down,
communicates nervousness
and superiority. Instead sit
down next to him or in front
of him, so you are literally
on the same level.

Opening lines

Good openers:

- "So what do you think of X (a film/band/mutual friend's new haircut)?"
- "So how do you know X?"

Don't be obsessed by chat
up lines. While it's good to be
creative about what you say,
if humour isn't your strong point,
just start with a normal
conversation opener. This always
works because we all already
know stock phrases are a sign
that someone wants to talk to us
but doesn't know how to start.

Learn to take
a compliment

How to accept a compliment:

- just say, "Thank you"
- or say, "What a nice thing to say"
- don't rush to give one back, unless
  you really want to.

The worst thing you can say
when someone gives you a
compliment is "Oh no I'm not"
or suggest they are just being nice.
Not only is it offensive to have a
compliment thrown back in your
face but it's also a signal that
you don't want to hear nice
things about yourself.

Use your brain

Tip – boys love to talk about themselves, but don't like emotional questions:

- don't say, "So were you heartbroken when X dumped you?"
- do say, "That film was cool. What did you like about it?"

It takes more than a pretty face to keep someone's attention, so always have some stock questions on hand before you go out. To keep the conversation going always ask open-ended questions that require more than a yes or no answer, and don't bombard him with hundreds of questions, you'll freak him out.

Don't be
negative

The biggest turn-off when you're flirting is to hear someone say endlessly negative things about themselves, their friends and their life. If you're a constant complainer, the message you're giving out is that it takes a lot to please you and you're hard work.

Don't sell
yourself short

Research shows:

- many women have such a poor body image that they underestimate their attractiveness by as much as 25%
- 80% of women believe they are too fat, and don't believe men will find them desirable.

The truth of the matter is
we're all fascinated (and horrified)
by our supposed flaws. The good
news is everyone is too busy
looking at themselves to really
notice the way your hair kinks,
that your eyebrows meet in the
middle, or the way your body
curves. So stop worrying because
the other weird irony is one
person's "flaw" is usually the thing
that draws people to them.

Don't
judge him
too harshly

So up close he isn't a love-god
with film star looks and
the banter of a comedian.
Unless he's uncouth and
rude, give him a chance.
Sometimes it takes a
while to see someone's
true personality and
inner charm.

Avoid
elevator eyes

As tempting as it is to check
out the other person while
flirting with them, no one likes
the once-over. This is when you
let your eyes travel like an elevator
from their head to their legs
and back up again. If you want
to look at them do it from a
distance and before they're
watching your every move.

Mirror him

Mirror musts:

- adopt the same volume and speed
  of speech that he's using
- use similar phrases and words
  that he's used
- sit in a similar fashion to him
- only copy positive body language.

Mirroring, as in repeating someone's words, body language and gestures, works because it subtly tells the person you're on their wavelength and so makes them feel immediately comfortable and open with you. Though be careful not to copy his every move otherwise he'll think you're bonkers!

Read him right

Look for groups of behaviour traits:

- if his arms are crossed, he's looking over your shoulder and ignoring what you say – he's not interested
- but if his arms are crossed, he's smiling and leaning in when you speak – he's interested.

Don't jump to conclusions
about his body language. Having
his arms crossed doesn't always
mean he's not open to you.
It could be a sign he's cold or in
a comfortable position. Looking
up to the left and avoiding your
gaze also doesn't mean he's
lying, he could just be shy
and embarrassed.

Tease him

Playful teasing (as in pulling
his leg) is a good way to flirt as
it allows you to get more personal
and intimate (and add some tactile
behaviour) without actually going
through the question and answer
process. Plus guys love pretend
arguments and fake insults as it
lightens the mood.

Charm school tips

Charm tactics:

- introduce him to your friends and repeat bits you've learned about him
- keep him involved in the conversation so he doesn't feel like a spare part
- if his friends come over, talk to them and dazzle them with your charm (but obviously don't flirt).

When flirting there are certain
things to remember. A guy is not
your property just because you're
chatting him up. This means don't
act like his girlfriend if another
girl approaches, don't be territorial
if your friends appear, and never
get huffy if he says he's got to
go back to his mates.

Don't flirt
with his friends

Okay you're on a flirt roll, you've won him over and he's hooked but you can confuse him totally (and lose him in the process) by turning your flirt beam on his friends. This will not only make him think you weren't serious about him but make his friends think you're bad news.

Use
your body

Body language is an essential
element of flirting. If you're out in
a group how you sit will affect how
boys respond to you. Use your
posture to signal your willingness
to flirt by sitting with your knees
or body pointed in the direction
of the object of your interest.
Use your hands as you talk to
gesture a person to look closer at
you, and pull your shoulders back
to show you're open and friendly.

Don't be
too eager

No matter how keen you are,
be subtle with your flirting.
Grabbing his hand as you speak,
laughing loudly at his jokes,
pushing your leg against his
and repeatedly telling him
he's fantastic is flirting overkill.
Calm down!

Avoid
fast flirting

Take time to find out:

- if he has a sense of humour about himself
- if you do actually want to go out with him
- whether you have things in common.

Tempting as it is to speed
from initial contact to kissing
and a date, putting all your cards
down within five minutes of
meeting is frightening even for
someone who is interested. Take
your time when you flirt, so you
can discover if this is about more
than animal attraction.

Give him
some attitude

After you've bypassed the initial
flirt stages of letting him know
you're interested, it pays to
give him some attitude. Not the
treat-him-mean-to-keep-him-keen
act but the this-is-who-I-am act.
Don't be afraid to disagree with
him, speak your mind, say what
you believe in. No one wants
to date a 'yes' girl.

Be tactile

Touch him to show that you like
him, but be careful where you go.
Faces are off limits to people who
don't know each other very well,
as are the obvious bodily areas.
But touching someone on the arm
as you speak, playfully pushing
their arm (gently) as you joke, and
if you're daring, touching their
knee, all say "I like you a lot".

Expose your secret zones

Secret zones:

- the inner wrist, and the inside upper arm
- ankles, feet, and inside calf muscle of your leg
- the nape of the neck.

It sounds strange but countless
body language studies show
that revealing areas of your
body that aren't usually on show
(no not your private bits) can
and does have an immediate effect
on the person you're flirting with,
as it shows them instantly that
you fancy them.

Get lippy

When we find ourselves attracted to someone, our lips naturally fill with blood and become lush and pouty in order to grab and hold the person's attention. To speed up the look think about adding a touch of gloss to the middle of your lower lip. This makes your lips look bigger and more irresistible to the guy you're flirting with.

Use
your hair

Contrary to popular opinion, flicking your hair irritates boys because they don't know what you're doing. To use your hair to its best advantage play with it as you talk. Twiddle it around your fingers. Lift it off your neck (an excellent ruse because it also shows off your neck), and run your fingers through it.

Let your
eyes sparkle

Eye tips:

- if you're shy, aim your focus at the space between his eyebrows and it will look as if you're staring into his eyes
- the more eye contact you establish the better. Glancing over his shoulder or around the room as he speaks signals that you're bored by him.

When we fancy someone our
eyes get bigger and our tear glands
start producing more moisture,
which gives our eyes that shiny
love struck glow. To let someone
see what your eyes are doing
be careful not to flutter your
eyelashes too much or look down
when you talk as it will hide
that sexy sparkle.

Be handy
with your
hands

Let your fingers play with your
rings, touch your lips or stroke the
rim of a glass and it will show him
you're playful as well as sweet.
Stroke the inside of your wrist
(a secret erogenous and sensual
zone), your palms or your knee
and you'll be saying, get-closer-
because-I-really-really-like-you.

Send clear
signals

Some guys read too much into
flirting signals so be clear about
what you're sending out to him.
If your aim is to see him again and
then decide if you like him, don't
get too close as this will make him
think you want more right now.
If you do want to kiss him, don't
back off when he leans in or else
he'll think you don't like him.

Work out his
space zone

- watch for when he moves back or flinches – this is too close for comfort
- aim to stay about two inches back from his space barrier as this is his perfect distance.

Before you move closer you need
to work out his personal space
zone. This is the area he feels
comfortable about letting you into.
In some cases this will be a
few inches, in others at least
arm's-length. A good way to
deduct this without freaking him
out is to pretend you haven't heard
what he says and move in slowly
as if you're trying to hear him.

Smile
sincerely

Spontaneous smiles that win over a person's affection are easy to spot so don't flash someone a fake one. To tell if he is flirting with his smile look for wrinkles around his eyes when he smiles (these won't appear if he's faking it) and a smile that naturally fades away, rather than lasts too long.

Don't overdo
the eye contact

This is also a common
mistake when flirting. Stare
into someone's eyes for too long
and you'll make them feel
uncomfortable and self-conscious.
The best way to use your eye
contact is to look at them while
they speak, and then glance
away now and again while
you're speaking.

Oversell
overkill

Don't go into sell overdrive.
While it's good to let the person
you fancy know you're an
attractive proposition, running
off a list of your exam results,
your measurements, your dancing
certificates and how many friends
you have will make you sound
arrogant, not interesting.

It's how you say it

Close is good because:

- it puts him firmly into your personal space, a sure sign that you fancy him
- it gives you the chance to really let your eyes do the talking.

When you're trying to win someone over don't stress about how intelligent or witty you sound, but think instead about your delivery. Talk LOUDLY... and your object of desire will back away, not only physically but mentally as well. Talk normally and he'll think you're just being friendly. Drop your tone and volume and he'll just have to move closer to hear you (sneaky but it works!).

Give
compliments

Flattery will get you everywhere
and countless studies prove it.
If you hear someone praising
or admiring you, your interest
in that person automatically
increases. However, keep
your compliments sincere.
People can spot a fake
compliment a mile off.

Say
his name

If you want to bond more quickly
with your flirt partner, use his
name at least twice in the
conversation. This shows that
you're paying attention and at the
same time it's a subtle signal that
you want to connect more
deeply with him.

Keep your
conversation
lively

Talking too slowly, pausing too
long and taking too long to make
your point is tedious for the other
person. Don't be in love with
the sound of your own voice.
You should speak for roughly the
same amount of time as the other
person unless you want them
to get quickly bored of you.

Don't be
self absorbed

You're being self absorbed when:

- instead of listening to him you're
  worrying about what he's thinking
- you can't remember the last two
  things he said
- you try to see your reflection in
  the glass you're holding.

If you're too busy worrying
what he thinks of you, or what
your tummy and/or hair looks
like, or even about the next thing
you're going to say, you won't be
able to flirt properly. To be an
effective flirt you need to keep
your wits about you and think
outwards not inwards.

Use your
memory

Listen to him. Studies
show remembering bits of
information about people you
like, and working them into
conversation, is not only highly
flattering but shows that firstly
you're interested because you've
paid attention, and secondly
you are someone worth
getting to know.

Give
something
back

If you want your conversation
to get more intimate and personal
give out a small detail about
yourself. If the person you're
flirting with likes you he will
give you an equally personal
titbit back. If you then add
further details, you can move
the conversation on to a more
private level.

Lighten up

Humour is the best tool to
get you a whole host of dates
and you don't have to be a
comedian to use it effectively.
We're not talking jokes,
but an ability to laugh at
the ridiculous. Show him
your lighter funnier side and
he'll want to see you again.

Make him
look at your
mouth

Dying to kiss him? Then draw attention to your lips. Either bite your bottom lip, lick your lips (be subtle), or rub your lips lightly as you speak. Better still start staring at his mouth when he talks. This will not only make him 100% conscious of his mouth and yours, but also hopefully give him the hint to do something with it.

Always
leave him
wanting more

Don't be tempted to spill all
your beans at once. When
you're flirting it pays to keep
him guessing. No guy needs to
know your cat's nickname, what
you've written in your diary
and how you're just 'desperate'
for a boyfriend. Mystery is
100 times more intriguing.

Back out
anytime
you want

Not all flirt specimens turn
out to be what you hoped for.
If Mr Gorgeous has turned into
Mr Crass, Mr Ego or even
Mr Two Timing Creep don't be
afraid to walk off and start again.
Think of flirting like shopping
for shoes – some look great in the
window, but feel awful when
you try them on. Don't worry –
somewhere out there is the
perfect fit for you.

Limit your
flirt time

It's time to go when:

- you're running out of flirt steam
- you're sure you've got him hooked
- you've made an arrangement to keep
  in contact.

A good way to keep him interested
is to leave at the height of your
flirt power. This not only takes
the pressure off you to be on your
best form but also allows him to
sit back and decide what he thinks
about you. However, don't just
disappear because he won't know
how to get in touch – make sure
you've at least swapped phone
numbers or email addresses.

To kiss or
not to kiss

Kissing is good flirtatious
behaviour if you want to reel him
in. However, we're not talking
about a full on snog. If you want
him to kiss you, try leaning over
and kissing him on the cheek when
he says something nice to you.
This is not only cheeky but says,
"Okay then what next?"

Fix up
another
meeting

Don't be afraid to take your
flirting to another level by
suggesting you meet up again,
especially if you're running out
of flirt steam and he hasn't
suggested anything. The easiest
way to do this is to pass him
your mobile number and simply
say, "Call me", or ask for his
email address. .

Don't plague him

- keeping in touch is – flirt texting him the next day to say you had fun, and then waiting for a reply before you do anything else
- stalking him is – sending him 3 emails, two texts and then calling him because you don't trust that he'll call you.

As tempting as it is to send him
a text or email every five minutes
DON'T! If you wouldn't call
him 14 times a day (and we're
hoping you won't) you shouldn't
stalk him by text. Annoy him
constantly and he'll erase
you from his speed dial.

Flirting
by phone

Phone flirting is hard especially as loads of guys simply use the phone as a tool to communicate details and not as a chatting device. If the guy you fancy acts 'weird' on the phone, don't freak out. It's likely he can't flirt without seeing your body language signals (very common) and can't tell what he's supposed to do or say just from your voice.

Flirting
by text

Text flirting is the easiest
way to flirt. However, thanks to
abbreviations and the length of
texts it's easy to take something
the wrong way or read too much
into a comment. Don't obsess
over what he means. If it's
bothering you, call him up
and ask him.

Flirting
by email

Email is as powerful as a
letter and a conversation so if
you wouldn't say it face to face
don't say it via computer. It's
a great way to initiate a date
but don't get so caught up in the
computer that when you finally
meet him it's awkward. Also
remember that it's often hard to
judge the tone of an email, and
once you've pressed the 'send'
button you can't take it back!

Don't sit
by the phone

You can ruin the confidence
boost of a good flirt by attaching
yourself to a phone and waiting
for him to call. The hard fact is
boys who are interested call!
So don't torture yourself with
what you did and didn't do and
whether he's lost your number.
Put it down to experience
and move on.

Show him
you've got a life

Good flirts:

- don't make his hobbies theirs.
  If you're going to get into football
  do it because you love it, not because
  it impresses blokes
- don't care if their interests are
  interesting to boys because they are
  doing it for themselves.

Don't be a girl who is so boy
obsessed she hasn't got a life.
The best flirts are girls who have
something to offer besides a pretty
face and successful flirts are girls
who can talk about other things
besides dating, boys and
er...boys.

Keep flirting

Flirting musts:

- tease your boyfriend – use your body language to get his attention at parties, and then move closer when he's least expecting it
- flirt just for the hell of it – even if you don't fancy someone it's fun to chat away to someone new. Who knows who you'll meet as a result!

Practice makes perfect with flirting and the only way to improve your technique is to use it absolutely everywhere and anytime (though only with appropriate people). Also remember that flirting is a skill to use in your relationship too, as it stops you from taking each other for granted.

What are you
waiting for?

Get flirting!